Queen of her Strom

AUTHOR NAME:-

<u>Rounakpreet kaur</u>

Part:-1

ISBN:
9798878293143

<u>DEDICATION</u>

This story isn't just mine. It's an anthem for every soul who's ever been broken, for everyone who's risen from the ashes. It's a testament to the human spirit's indomitable will, the unwavering love that binds us, and the strength we find within ourselves, even when the world throws its worst.

Remember, dear reader, you are not alone. Scars tell stories, not of fragility, but of resilience. Let them be your armor, your reminder that you have weathered storms and emerged stronger. Keep rising, keep fighting, keep loving. You are the author of your own epic, and your greatest chapters are yet to be written.

CONTENTS

ACKNOWLEDGMENTS

This book is for you. I hope you find something within its pages that resonates with you and leaves a lasting impression.

1 CHAPTER NAME

TEENY

My childhood was painted with love, thanks to my incredible parents. But it was my dad who truly earned the title of "World's Best Dad." Why? Because his support knew no bounds. Before I even entered the world, tragedy struck: my grandmother passed away from breast cancer. My arrival, instead of a boy as everyone expected, could have been a disappointment. Yet, Dad's face lit up. As he never got disappointed on me. He chose my name, whose meaning is "happiness," and it symbolized his joy at my birth.

However, my childhood dreams , big or small, became his missions. As

At three, I craved a mango in the end of summer season and it was expensive(800rupee),Despite the cost, he brought it home, his sacrifice a testament to his boundless love. Another time, my tears demanded a kite-flying under the twinkling night sky. Even after a long day, Dad climbed onto the roof, our laughter echoing in the darkness

But his love went beyond whims. He harbored a dream—to see his child playing tennis, inspired by his admiration for Steffi Graf. With me, his first child, this dream ignited. He wasn't just a supporter; he became my coach, my cheerleader, my rock .

My childhood wasn't

perfect, but it was filled with a father's unwavering love. He saw potential where others saw limitations, celebrating every victory and comforting every tear. This story isn't just about me; it's about the transformative power of a father's belief, a love that shapes my dreams and paves the path to fulfillment.

As time ticked by, days turned into weeks, weeks into months, and months into years. I blossomed from a curious toddler into a nervous little student. Today marked a momentous occasion - my first day of school! Excitement buzzed in the air, but it was overshadowed by a knot of fear in my stomach. This sprawling building, filled with unknown faces and routines, felt colossal and lonely. I yearned for the familiar warmth of my parents' hands at my side.

My mom, her eyes

mirroring my anxieties, struggled to let go. Her smile trembled, and I could see the unspoken promise in her gaze, "I'll be right back." Dad, usually the pillar of strength, stood a little taller, his chin held high, but a tear glistening on his cheek betrayed his hidden emotions. They both knelt before me, their voices laced with love and reassurance.

"This is a big day, sweetheart," Mom said, wiping my tear with a gentle thumb. "But remember, you're brave and capable. Make new friends, explore, and learn all you can!"

Dad, his voice thick with emotion, added, "We'll be waiting right here when school ends. And hey, we will eat your favorite dessert.

Their words, laced with love and faith, Taking a deep breath, I squeezed my hands ,a silent promise to conquer my fears. With a final hug, they waved goodbye, their smiles etched in my memory and Stepping through the school doors, I felt a wave of uncertainty wash over me. But then, I remembered their encouraging words, the love in their eyes. With a newfound resolve, I took a small step forward, ready to embark on this exciting new chapter knowing their love would guide me every step of the way.

2 CHAPTER NAME

SCHOOL AGE

The morning sun streamed through the window, painting golden stripes across the room where Rounak slumbered. Her dreams were filled with adventures on her father's motorbike, her hair whipping in the wind as she raced towards a new day. But soon, the gentle voice of her mother, Rounak, calling her to wake up, brought her back to reality.

Rounak was in her first-grade

and   Forget neat lines in a notebook or agonizing over spelling tests - Rounak was the queen of the playground , as she has lot of love for sports. She was active participant in sports.

Her laughter echoed like wind chimes on a sunny day, braids flying as she weaved through games of tag. Her heart held the warmth of a thousand suns, her smile could melt glaciers, and her love for everyone she met radiated like sunshine.

  where as , academics became a different story. numbers waltzed before her eyes in a dizzying blur, and alphabets jumbled into nonsensical puzzles. despite her mother's patient guidance and gentle prodding, report cards more often reflected her struggles than successes. yet, whenever discouragement threatened to dim her sparkle, her father, Sardar Gurpinder Singh, would swoop in, his booming laughter and playful challenges rekindling the spark within. he'd remind Rounak of her true superpowers: the unwavering kindness that made her everyone's friend, the natural leadership that made her shine in games, and the infectious enthusiasm that brought joy to everything she did.

In the classroom, Ms. Patel became Rounak anchor. seeing beyond the report cards, Ms. Patel recognized the vibrant spirit bubbling within Rounak with her encouragement, Rounak blossomed, the classroom transforming into a stage where her imagination danced and soared.

life then presented a new chapter. a tiny bundle of joy named Amrinder Singh arrived, filling their home with gurgles and giggles. Rounak, initially unsure, was soon captivated by her baby brother. Amrinder became her confidante.

My brother grow up, my parents

made a decision to enroll my brother in a school known for its focus on skills development, activity, and intellectual growth. it seemed like the perfect environment for him to flourish. naturally, I assumed I'd follow suit. however, to my surprise, my father had a different plan. he believed I would also thrive in that environment, and decided I would join my brother at the same school. this unexpected change left me with a mix of emotions, curious about the new opportunities but also unsure of what to expect.

3 CHAPTER NAME

NEW SCHOOL

My first day at **MOUNT LITERA ZEE SCHOOL** was a whirlwind of nervous excitement. new faces, a new teacher, even the principal made an appearance! little did i know, this school would become my launchpad for academic and athletic achievements, forging lifelong friendships along the way. **MOUNT LITERA ZEE** wasn't just a school; it was a springboard for my sporting dreams. the supportive environment, nurtured by teachers, family, and friends, helped mc blossom into a champion, collecting medals

and trophies like souvenirs of countless victories.
my classmates...oh, what a crew! we were more than friends; we were a band of brothers and sisters, forging memories etched in laughter, tears, and shared secrets. we fought, we celebrated, we even played matchmaker for each other's love lives! these bonds transcended classrooms, lasting even when tournaments took me across the city. my friends wouldn't let me fall behind, diligently filling my

notebooks to ensure i stayed on top of academics. though math wasn't my forte, teachers and classmates never hesitated to lend a helping hand. those were the golden years, woven with triumphs and support, etched in my mind as the best memories of my life. but as 2019 dawned, things took a turn.

4 CHAPTER NAME

TRAGEDY

My heart aches as I recall the immense difficulties my father faced. He battled not only everyday struggles but also a persistent cough, concerning bleeding, and a series of tests. Then came the devastating news: thyroid cancer. The weight of that diagnosis pressed down on all of us, creating a palpable tension that demanded a delicate balance of positivity and realism. We rallied together, my family and I, determined to be his source of strength, whispering promises of victory despite the fear gnawing at our hearts.

He truly was the strongest person I knew. His fight was long and arduous, coinciding with my crucial board exams. My mother spent nights by his hospital bedside, offering unwavering support, while I and my brother soldiered on at home, juggling studies with the gnawing worry that consumed us. My friend Nancy's companionship during that isolating time was a lifeline, a beacon of normalcy amidst the storm. Yet, focusing on exams felt impossible under the crushing weight of our circumstances.

&

THE SURGERY, A DAUNTING PROSPECT TO SAY THE LEAST, WAS

THANKFULLY SUCCESSFUL. BUT THE JOY OF HIS RECOVERY WAS SHORT-LIVED AS THE CANCER RETURNED, demanding another grueling battle. For four years, he confronted this deadly disease with unwavering courage, enduring countless treatments that etched his body with the marks of his resilience. He emerged victorious, only to be dealt another blow, a new condition that inflicted unimaginable pain. Witnessing his suffering was deeply agonizing, the treatment a cruel reminder of the toll his strength had taken.

TRAGEDY

5 CHAPTER NAME

TURNING POINT

THE NEWS OF YOUR FATHER'S PASSING HANGS HEAVY IN THE AIR, ITS WEIGHT PRESSING DOWN ON YOUR WORDS, PAINTING THEM WITH RAW GRIEF. THE IMAGE OF YOUR FATHER'S FIGHT, A VALIANT

WARRIOR BATTLING A RELENTLESS FOE, PIERCES THE HEART. HIS UNEXPECTED LOSS AT 5:10 AM, a time when the world should be waking to promise, instead plunged you into a chilling darkness.

A FATHER, THE ANCHOR OF A FAMILY, THE ONE WHO HOLDS THE SKY, GONE. THE ATMOSPHERE, THICK WITH THE SUFFOCATING STING OF LOSS, MIRRORED THE

VOID LEFT WITHIN YOU. TEARS, PERHAPS UNSPOKEN PROMISES WHISPERED TO THE WIND, A DESPERATE ATTEMPT TO GRASP AT WHAT SLIPPED AWAY.

His diary, a treasure trove of wisdom and love, became a lifeline in the storm. His final wish, "do not cry, become strong as no one can become, be your own shoulder and never let your mother down" a poignant plea echoing in the hollowness, a burden weighing heavily on your young shoulders. Yet, you rose, becoming the rock for your grieving mother and brother, a testament to the strength he instilled in you.

But anger, a bitter counterpoint to sorrow, flickers in your words. Uncle and aunt, painted as villains in the tapestry of your grief, their actions cast as the harbingers of your father's suffering. His pain, fueled by betrayal and unspoken love, a wound festering in his kind heart. Tears he shed in secret, a silent testament to the burdens he carried alone.

His death, a seismic shift, shattering the world you knew. Everything changed, leaving you adrift in a sea of uncertainty. Yet, amidst the wreckage, a flicker of determination emerges. You, too, are changing, evolving into the person your father always knew you could be.

R

I should have
hugged you tighter
and longer
the last time
I saw you

To be Continued.

(part-2 on way).

Waheguru

Waheguru

33
R

Waheguru

Waheguru

Waheguru

Waheguru

Waheguru

Waheguru

Waheguru

Waheguru

Waheguru

Waheguru

Waheguru

Waheguru

Waheguru

Waheguru

Waheguru

Waheguru

Waheguru

Waheguru

Waheguru

Waheguru

53
R

Waheguru

Waheguru

55
R

Waheguru

Waheguru

Waheguru

Waheguru

Waheguru

Waheguru

Waheguru

Waheguru

Waheguru

64

R

Waheguru

Waheguru

Waheguru

Waheguru

Waheguru

R

Waheguru

Waheguru

Waheguru

Waheguru

Waheguru

Waheguru

ABOUT THE AUTHOR

Twenty years old, yet her eyes held the weight of worlds witnessed. Curiosity, insatiable and sharp, propelled her forward, a constant seeker of understanding amidst the ever-shifting sands of global chaos. Stability, a distant promise glimpsed in fleeting moments, yet never fully grasped. The scars of experience, woven into the fabric of her being, whispered tales of resilience and heartbreak, a testament to a spirit unafraid to delve into the depths of life's tapestry. This young woman, an author in the making, was poised to capture the world's complexities with a pen poised and a heart brimming with stories waiting to be told.